HOW THINGS WORK!

MUSICAL INSTRUMENTS

ADE DEANE-PRATT

PowerKiDS
press™

New York

Published in 2012 by The Rosen Publishing Group Inc.
29 East 21st Street, New York, NY 10010

First Edition

Editors: Rob Colson and Jennifer Sanderson
Consultant: Penny Johnson
Step-by-step photography: Ed Simkins, Caroline Watson
Designer: Jonathan Vipond

Library of Congress Cataloging-in-Publication Data

Deane-Pratt, Ade.
Musical instruments / by Ade Deane-Pratt. -- 1st ed.
    p. cm. -- (How things work)
Includes index.
ISBN 978-1-4488-5280-2 (library binding)
1. Musical instruments--Juvenile literature. 2. Musical instruments--Construction--Juvenile literature. I. Title.
ML460.D47 2012
784.19--dc22

2010046538

Web Sites

Due to the changing nature of Internet links, PowerKids Press has developed an online list of Web sites related to the subject of this book. This site is updated regularly. Please use this link to access this list: http://www.powerkidslinks.com/htw/music/

Photographs:
(t) top; (c) center; (b) bottom; (l) left; (r) right
1 and 9 (b) Clive Chilvers/Dreamstime.com; 2 and 15 (tr) Mario Curcio/Dreamstime.com; 4 Sebastian Czapnik/ Dreamstime.com; 5 Ferenc Szelepcsenyi/Shutterstock. com; (l) Sonbeam/Dreamstime.com, (c) Mark Fairey/ Dreamstime.com, (r) Bart Coenders; 9 (tl) Wayland, (tr) Dmitry Skutin/Dreamstime.com; 11 (t) Dennis Tokarzewski/Dreamstime.com, (c) Bernd Juergens/ Dreamstime.com, (b) Beata Pastuszek/iStock; 12 Wikipedia Commons; 13 (tl) Craig Hanson/Dreamstime. com, (tr) Wikipedia Commons, (b) Monkey Business Images/Dreamstime.com; 15 (c) Lehakok/Dreamstime. com, (b) Rick Lord/Dreamstime.com; 16 Heike Brauer | Dreamstime.com; 17 (t) Heike Brauer/Dreamstime.com, (c) Cagri Oner/iStock, (b) Cathyclapper/Dreamstime. com; 19 (tl) Ang Wee Heng John/Dreamstime.com, (tr) Sean Prior/Dreamstime.com, (bl) Eagleflying/ Dreamstime.com, (br) Dmitriy Cherevko/Dreamstime. com, 21 (tr) Oleg Prikhodko/iStock, (c) Jeremyrichards/ Dreamstime.com, (b) Nicholas Sutcliffe/shutterstock.com

Manufactured in China
CPSIA Compliance Information: Batch #WAS1102PK: For Further Information contact Rosen Publishing, New York, New York at 1-800-237-9932

CONTENTS

SOUNDS AND MUSIC

Music is a sequence of sounds and we can make music by singing and playing different instruments. We can bang them, blow into them, pluck them, or bow them to produce a wide range of sounds.

MAKING MUSIC

Sounds are made by vibrations that travel through the air, through liquids, and even through solids, such as walls. You cannot see these vibrations, but your ears can pick them up. Sounds become music when they are organized into patterns of notes. Music can be made with our voices, or it can be made using a musical instrument.

This musician is playing a guitar. He plucks the strings to make them vibrate, which in turn makes sounds. A sequence of sounds produces a melody.

A RANGE OF SOUNDS

Instruments sound different from each other because of the way they change three features of musical notes: volume, pitch, and timbre (pronounced tom-brer). Volume is how loud or soft a sound is. The pitch of a sound is how high or low it is. Sounds also have a different "feel" or quality to them. This is the note's timbre.

This book looks at different groups of instruments, including percussion, string, woodwind, and brass. The project pages will show you how to make your own instruments.

An orchestra is a large group of people playing different instruments at the same time. This large orchestra includes violins, cellos, horns, and trombones.

SHAKING AND SCRAPING

Instruments that make a sound when we hit, shake, or scrape them are called percussion instruments. They set the pace of music and keep the rhythm. Shakers and scrapers make a huge variety of sounds—they rattle, jangle, rasp, and clatter.

HOW DOES IT WORK?

Scrapers are instruments that have one or more ridges. Musicians use a stick to stroke over the ridges, which makes a sound. Shakers are made from a container that is either filled with seeds or has beads around the outside. For example, maracas are made from a hollow container filled with seeds or rice. When you shake a maraca, the seeds hit the container and make it vibrate. This makes the air inside the maraca vibrate to produce the sound. The timbre of shakers and scrapers depends on the material from which they are made—for instance, leather shakers produce "warmer" sounds than plastic ones.

güiro

stick scrapes over grooves to produce sound

vibrations produce sound

seeds hit inside of container when maracas are shaken

maraca

Try it !

Take an empty container with a lid. Pour in some rice, put the lid on firmly, and then shake it. Now try it again with some metal screws instead of rice. How has the timbre of the sound changed?

SHAKERS AND SCRAPERS IN ACTION

Shakers and scrapers are played all over the world. The material from which they are made often comes from local plants and trees.

A rainstick is a shaker made from the stem of a cactus plant with small pebbles inside. It sounds like falling rain when you turn it upside down.

Güiros are scrapers originally from Latin America. They are played by rubbing a stick up and down over the grooves.

The shekere is a West African shaker made from a container covered with beads woven into a net. The beads hit the container to make a sound when the shekere is twisted or shaken.

BEATING A RHYTHM

Drums are a type of percussion instrument. You can beat them with a stick, a brush, or your hands. They are often used to keep a regular beat while other instruments play a tune over them.

HOW DOES IT WORK?

Drums are made of a skin stretched over the top of an empty container, called a shell. The skin vibrates when it is hit and makes the air inside the drum vibrate with it. If the skin is stretched tightly, the drum will have a high pitch. The volume and timbre of a drum are affected by the size and shape of the container, and also by the way the drum is hit. Banging a drum with a hand makes a softer sound than banging it with a drumstick.

Try it !

Take an empty container, such as a metal can with a lid on it. Hit the lid with your hand and listen to the sound. Now put some sand inside the container and hit it again. How has the sound changed?

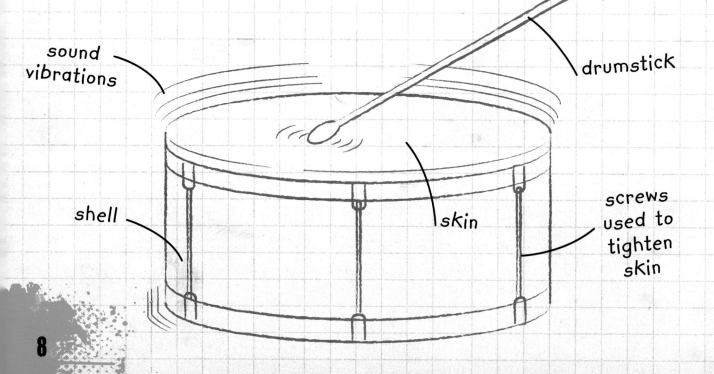

sound vibrations

drumstick

shell

skin

screws used to tighten skin

8

middle tom

crash cymbal

The timpani, or kettle drum, is a large drum that is often played in an orchestra. It is played using a special stick called a timpani mallet, which has a large head covered in soft felt.

Drum kits (or drum sets) are made up of drums of different sizes. This kit includes crash cymbals and middle toms.

DRUMS IN ACTION

Drums are used in most styles of music, from rock to folk music. The kind of drum used depends on the type of music—for example, steel drums are used in the music from Trinidad, while bongo drums give Cuban music its rhythm.

There can be hundreds of drummers in a Brazilian samba band. The band uses lots of different sizes of drum. Each size of drum has a different pitch.

STRING INSTRUMENTS

Guitars, cellos, double basses, and violins are string instruments. They often make up the largest section in an orchestra because it takes many strings to create a rich sound.

HOW DOES IT WORK?

All string instruments are made from the same main parts—strings, a bridge, tuning pegs, and a body. Plucking or bowing strings makes them vibrate to produce notes. On a guitar, the strings are fixed to a tuning peg at the top of the fingerboard, and then stretched over the sound hole and the bridge. The sound hole amplifies the sound, making it louder.

Thick, loose strings produce the lowest notes, while thin, tight strings make the highest. You can make a string's pitch higher by using the tuning peg to wind it tighter. You also make the pitch higher by pressing the string onto the fingerboard. This makes the string shorter. Shorter strings vibrate faster to make higher-pitched notes.

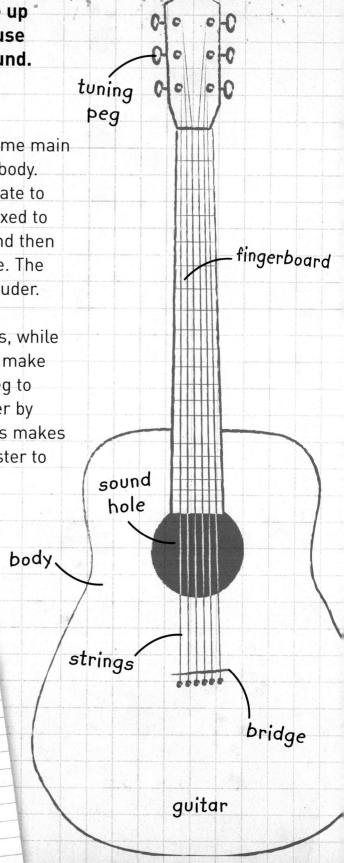

tuning peg

fingerboard

sound hole

body

strings

bridge

guitar

Try it !

Stretch a rubber band between the forefinger and thumb of one hand. Use your other hand to pluck the band, and listen. Is the sound it makes high or low pitched? What happens to the pitch if you stretch the band more tightly?

A cello is usually played using a bow. The strings are arranged in an arc so that the cellist can play only one or two strings at the same time.

STRINGS IN ACTION

The number of strings varies depending on the instrument: some guitars have six strings, a cello has four, and a sitar can have 23. Plucking strings makes notes short and sharp. Using a bow can produce long, continuous notes.

Guitarists can play more than one note at a time. Notes played together like this are called a chord. Musicians play the chord by strumming the strings with one hand and by pressing them against the fingerboard using the other. This produces notes with different pitches that sound good together.

Sitars originally come from India. They have two layers of strings and a wide, sloping bridge that give these instruments their unique sound.

PIANOS AND KEYBOARDS

Pianos have strings that are played using a keyboard. Keyboard instruments produce notes either by striking or plucking a string to make it vibrate, or by causing air to flow through a pipe.

HOW DOES IT WORK?

A piano keyboard has 88 keys. Each key plays a different string inside the piano. When the pianist presses a key, a hammer hits the string to make it vibrate. Hitting a key harder causes the strings to vibrate more, creating a louder note. When the key is released, a block, called a damper, drops onto the string to stop it vibrating. Pianists can use a foot pedal to hold the dampers up, so that the notes keep going after the keys have been released.

Try it !

Stretch a rubber band between the forefinger and thumb of one hand. Pluck the band gently to make a sound, and then pluck it harder. Which sound is louder? Can you see how the size of the vibration increases the harder you pluck?

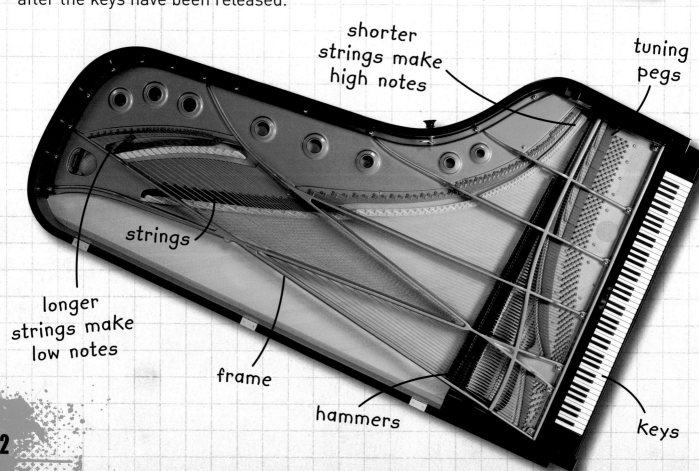

shorter strings make high notes

tuning pegs

strings

longer strings make low notes

frame

hammers

keys

Harpsichords look similar to pianos, but they are different inside. Instead of being hit by a hammer, the strings are plucked by small picks that are operated by the keys.

An organ produces notes by making the air inside pipes vibrate. Longer organ pipes produce lower-pitched notes. The largest organs have pipes up to 66 feet (20 meters) long.

KEYBOARDS IN ACTION

All keyboard instruments can play several notes at once. The instruments are either played on their own as solo instruments, or they are used to accompany a group of musicians or a choir.

An upright piano is smaller than a grand piano because the strings are arranged vertically. It still plays the same range of notes.

BLOWING BRASS

Brass instruments include trumpets, tubas, trombones, and French horns. They are played by blowing air into a mouthpiece shaped like a cup or a funnel.

HOW DOES IT WORK?

The hollow part of a brass instrument is tube-shaped and filled with air. Brass players make the tube of air inside their instrument vibrate by "blowing a raspberry" into the mouthpiece. The pitch of the note changes depending on the length of the vibrating tube of air, in the same way as the note on a string instrument changes with the string's length.

A trombone player uses a slider to change the length of the tube of air. When the slider is out, the tube is longer. Longer tubes of vibrating air produce lower-pitched notes. Trumpet players press keys to open a valve in order to change the length of the tube of air. The large, flared end of brass instruments, called the bell, directs the sound toward the audience.

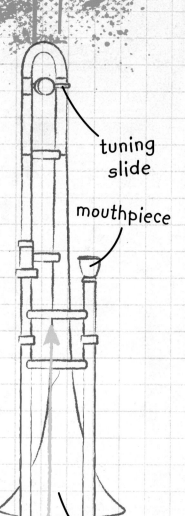

tuning slide

mouthpiece

bell

main slide moves in and out to change the length of the tube of air

trombone

Try it !

Roll up a square piece of card so that it makes a cone shape. Speak through the narrow end of the cone. How does it make your voice sound? Can other people hear you better if they stand in front of the cone or to one side?

BRASS IN ACTION

Most brass instruments are made from metal, but the alpine horn is a "brass" instrument made from wood. Brass instruments come in many different sizes. Larger instruments have a longer tube of air, so they make lower-pitched sounds. The tuba is the lowest brass instrument.

Alpine horns can be several yards long and make a very low-pitched sound. They were originally developed to help people to communicate across the Alps.

Marching bands combine small instruments, such as cornets, to play the high notes, with large instruments, such as tubas, to play the low notes.

The pitch of a trumpet is determined by opening and closing the valves and tightening or loosening the lips.

WOODWIND INSTRUMENTS

Flutes, oboes, and panpipes are all woodwind instruments. They have a hollow, tube-shaped body called a windpipe.

HOW DOES IT WORK?

A woodwind instrument makes a sound when the tube of air inside the windpipe vibrates. With oboes, clarinets, and saxophones, the air vibrates when a reed fixed to the mouthpiece vibrates. The musician makes the reed vibrate by blowing through it. Along the body of the instrument are holes that the player can close by covering them with a finger. This changes the length of the vibrating tube of air inside the windpipe, altering the pitch of the note.

Short pipes make high notes

wooden frame holds pipes together

musician blows into top of windpipes

Panpipes are a set of windpipes of different lengths. These do not have holes along them. Instead, each windpipe makes just one note.

Try it !

Take a glass bottle and half-fill it with water. Now blow across the mouth of the bottle so that it plays a note. What happens to the pitch of the sound if you pour out some of the water?

long pipes make low notes

Saxophones are single-reed instruments. The reed is made from dried cane or plastic.

WOODWIND IN ACTION

The timbre of a woodwind instrument depends on how the vibrations are made inside the instrument—either a single or double vibrating reed or by the player blowing into the instrument through a hole. It also depends on the shape of the instrument and what it is made from. Some woodwind instruments, such as saxophones and flutes, are actually made from metal rather than wood.

Oboes use a double reed to make vibrations. The windpipe has several keys that are pressed to cover different holes. This changes the note that is played.

Flute players hold the instrument out to the side as they play. Instead of blowing into the instrument, they blow across the hole at one end.

SINGING A SONG

Your voice can make many different sounds. Most often, you use your voice to speak, but you can also sing. You can change the volume, pitch, and timbre of your voice by changing the shape of your mouth.

HOW DOES IT WORK?

Your nose, mouth, throat, and lungs all help to produce the sound of your voice. When you breathe in, air moves down through your throat and into your lungs. When you breathe out again, air is squeezed back up through your throat. The moving air makes the vocal cords in your voice box vibrate. The pitch of your voice depends on the length and tightness of your vocal cords. Longer, looser vocal cords make lower-pitched sounds than shorter, tighter ones. Sounds are made louder when air vibrates in the spaces inside your nose and mouth.

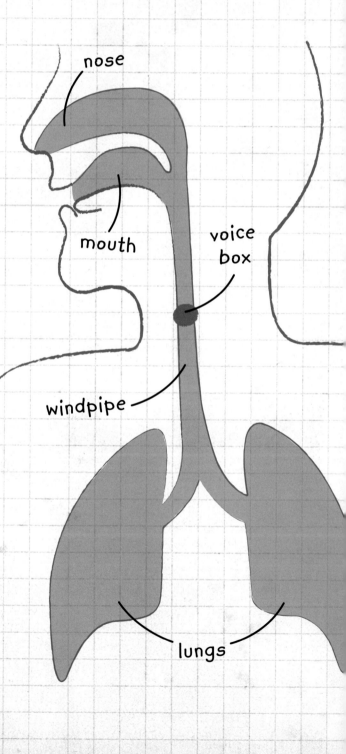

nose

mouth

voice box

windpipe

lungs

Try it !

Sing a note. Now sing the same note again, but this time pinch your nose. How does the note sound different?

Forcing air out of our lungs very quickly makes sounds louder, so that we can shout. When we whisper, our vocal cords vibrate only a little, so the sound is much quieter.

VOICES IN ACTION

When you sing a song, and even when you talk, the pitch of your voice moves up and down. You control the pitch with muscles in your throat, which loosen or tighten the vocal cords. You change the timbre of the sound by changing the shape of your mouth. With a lot of practice, singers can train their throat muscles to produce a wide range of notes from low to high pitch.

Changing the shape of the mouth changes the timbre of the sound. The person in the top photograph is saying "aah," and the person at the bottom is saying "ooh."

Choirs are divided into sections, with each section singing a different pitch to form the tune. In this choir, the women form one section and the men another. Women's voices are higher than men's because they have shorter vocal cords.

PUTTING IT TOGETHER

Different types of instrument can be combined into a group playing various kinds of music. These groups range from duets, with just two musicians, to large orchestras.

HOW DOES IT WORK?

In an orchestra, the musicians sit according to how loud their instruments are. Sound becomes quieter the farther away you are from the instrument making it. As a result, loud instruments are positioned at the back so that they do not drown out the other instruments. The conductor stands in a central position at the front of the orchestra. He or she ensures that the musicians all play in the correct time.

Try it !

Put the drums, shaker, bottles, and rubber bands that you used earlier in order from the quietest instrument to the loudest. How would you arrange them in an orchestra so that you could hear each instrument?

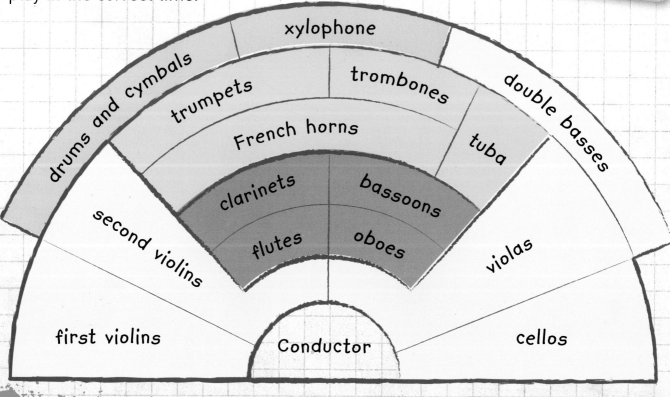

xylophone

drums and cymbals

trumpets

trombones

double basses

French horns

tuba

clarinets

bassoons

flutes

oboes

second violins

violas

first violins

Conductor

cellos

☐ Percussion   ☐ Brass   ☐ Woodwind   ☐ String

MUSICAL GROUPS IN ACTION

Different instruments in a group give the music its rhythm, play the main tune (the melody), or play the sounds that support the main tune, called harmonies. For some types of music, a group of musicians will support a solo player or a singer.

A large drum kit provides the rhythm to a rock song. The other instruments, such as electric guitars and bass guitars, combine to provide the main tune for the lead singer.

These performers use a pungi (back left) and a harmonium (front left) to create a traditional Indian sound.

This string quartet has four musicians: two playing violins, one playing a viola, and the other playing a cello. String quartets play a type of music called chamber music.

Make a Cardboard Guitar

Use this simple guitar to strum or pluck a tune. Can your friends guess what you are playing?

What you need

- shoebox
- paints and brushes
- compass
- sharp pencil
- scissors
- glue
- ten paper fasteners
- five long rubber bands

1 Decorate your shoebox using the paints and brushes.

2 Use the compass to draw a circle about 6 in. (15 cm) in diameter on the lid of the box. The circle should be closer to one end of the lid than the other. Ask an adult to cut out the circle.

3 Take the circle that has been cut from the lid and fold it along two parallel lines 1.5 in. (3 cm) apart. Then cut five slits into each side so that there are corresponding grooves on both ends.

1.5 in. (3 cm)

fold up

fold up

4 Glue the flat side of the folded circle onto the lid at the edge of the hole. Make sure the grooved edges are facing upward. This will be the guitar's bridge.

5 Turn the lid upside down. Using the pencil, poke five holes 2 in. (5 cm) apart in the rim at one end of the lid. Do the same at the other end of the lid, making sure that the holes at either end line up.

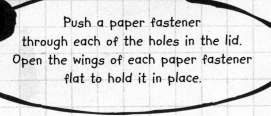

6 Push a paper fastener through each of the holes in the lid. Open the wings of each paper fastener flat to hold it in place.

7 Cut each rubber band in one place. These are your strings. Wind one end of a rubber band around a paper fastener. Pull the rubber band over the bridge, into the grooves, and attach it to the fastener at the other end of the lid. Do the same for each of the five rubber bands to secure the strings.

Take it further

- Tighten and loosen the strings. How does this change the notes?
- Try using a mixture of thick and thin rubber bands. Do they sound different?

8 Finally, put the lid back on the shoebox and pluck the strings using your fingers.

Make a Set of Panpipes

Panpipes are woodwind instruments often played in folk bands. Use drinking straws to make your own set of pipes.

3 in. (8 cm)

8 in. (20 cm)

What you need

- adhesive-backed plastic
- scissors
- ruler
- eight long, wide drinking straws

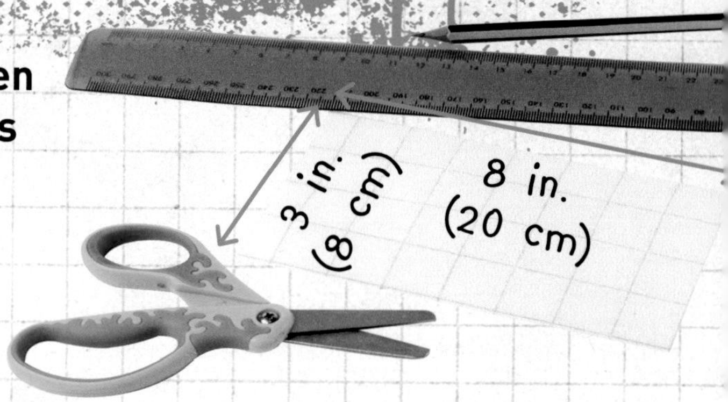

Draw a rectangle on the adhesive-backed plastic that is 3 in. (8 cm) wide and 8 in. (20 cm) long. Cut out the rectangle.

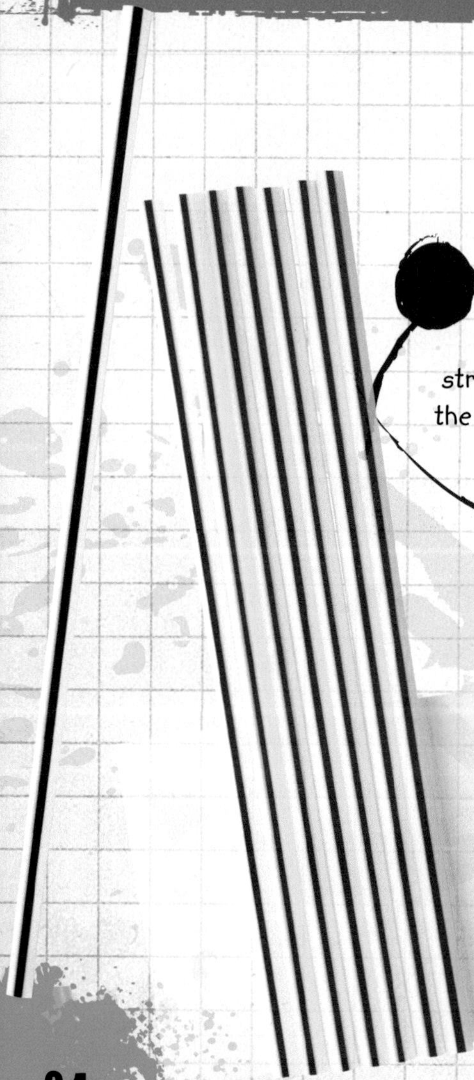

Peel the backing off the adhesive-backed plastic. Place the straws next to each other at one end of the sticky side. Make sure that the ends of the straws are right on the edge of the plastic.

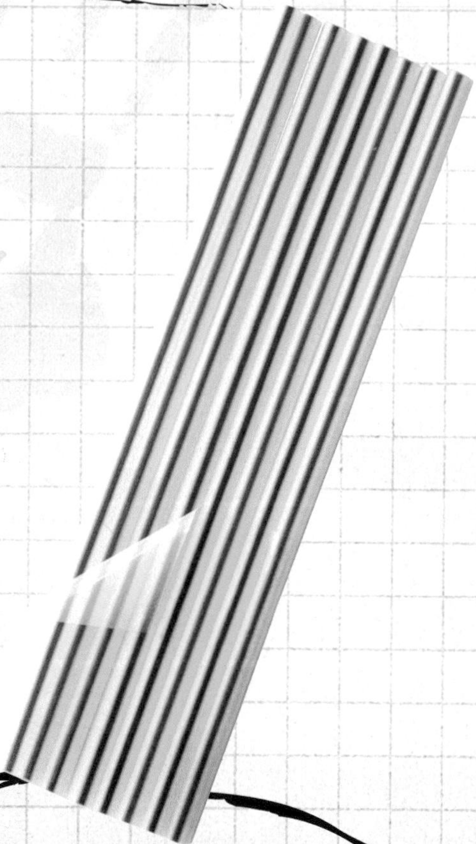

Carefully wrap the adhesive-backed plastic around the straws to hold them together.

To create different notes, cut the straw at one end in half. Then cut the straw next to it so that it is slightly longer. Then cut the third straw so that it is longer than the second one. Repeat this with all the straws. You should end up with the straws going from short to long.

Blow across the tops of the pipes to make a tune. Which straws produce the highest notes?

Take it further

- You can make the pitch of the pipes higher by cutting off small pieces from the bottom to shorten the straws.
- Try to make a set of panpipes with a larger range of notes.

Make a Drum

Percussion instruments add the beat or rhythm to music. Follow these steps and you will be beating out your own music.

tape

What you need

- round cookie can
- strong tape, such as packing tape
- scissors
- ruler
- cardboard
- double-sided tape
- paints and brushes
- two pencils with erasers at one end

1 To make the skin of the drum, cut a piece of tape that is longer than the can's diameter. Stick it across the center of the can.

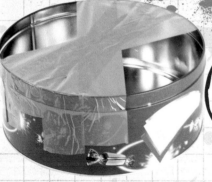

2 Cut another piece of tape as long as the first piece. Stick it over the previous piece to make an "X" on the can. Continue to stick tape over the can until the top is completely covered.

3 Use the ruler to measure the height of the side of the can. Cut a strip of card as wide as the height measurement and long enough to go around the can. Use double-sided tape to stick it to the can.

4 Paint the side of the drum to decorate it.

5 Use two pencils as drumsticks and tap the rubber ends against the drum skin. Does the sound have a low pitch or a high pitch?

Take it further

- Make more drums using larger and smaller cans. How does the sound of the drums differ?
- Use the other end of the pencils to play your drum. How does the sound change when you use the writing end to hit the drum skin, rather than the rubber end?

Make an Oboe

An oboe is a woodwind instrument that makes sounds using a double vibrating reed. You can make your own oboe using a straw and a cardboard tube.

What you need

- long, thin cardboard tube, such as the inner tube of tinfoil
- paints and brushes
- sharp pencil
- scissors
- plastic drinking straw
- modeling clay

1 Use the paint to decorate the cardboard tube. This will be the main body of your oboe.

2 in. (5 cm)

2 When the paint is dry, make five marks down the side of the tube about 2 in. (5 cm) apart. Carefully use the pencil to push holes through the tube on the marks.

cut here

reed

3 Cut the straw so it is about 4 in. (10 cm) long. Squash one end of the straw and cut a pointed "V" shape into the flattened end, as shown. This will be the double reed for your oboe.

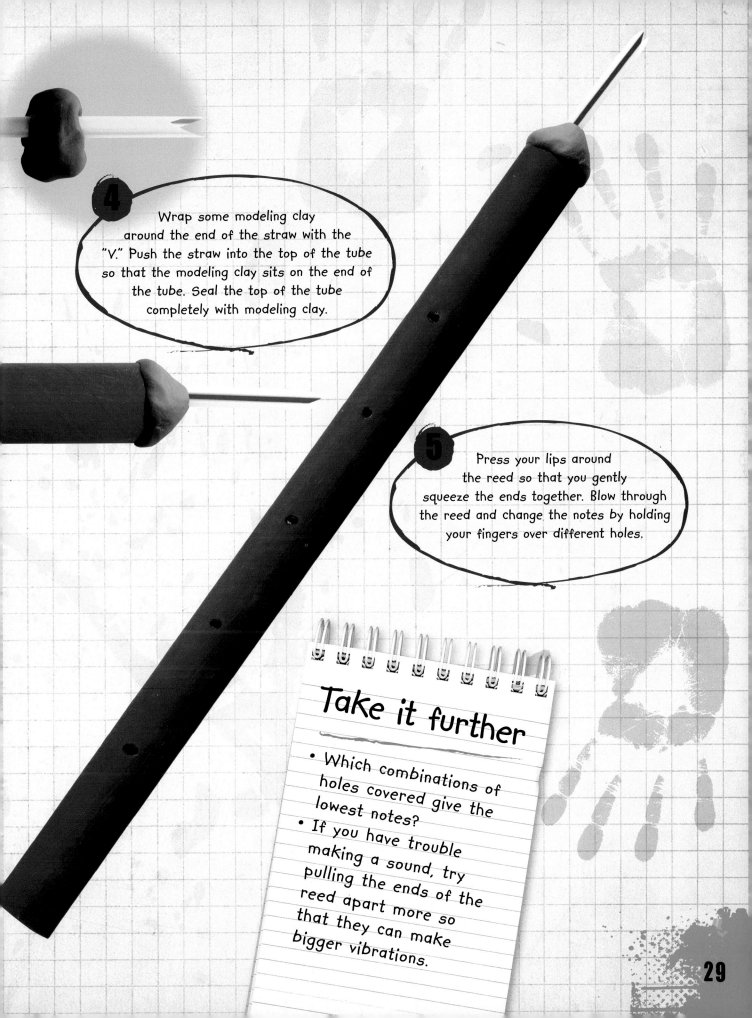

4 Wrap some modeling clay around the end of the straw with the "V." Push the straw into the top of the tube so that the modeling clay sits on the end of the tube. Seal the top of the tube completely with modeling clay.

5 Press your lips around the reed so that you gently squeeze the ends together. Blow through the reed and change the notes by holding your fingers over different holes.

Take it further

- Which combinations of holes covered give the lowest notes?
- If you have trouble making a sound, try pulling the ends of the reed apart more so that they can make bigger vibrations.

GLOSSARY

bow
A long, thin piece of wood with hair from a horse's tail stretched from one end to another. It is used to play string instruments.

brass instruments
Musical instruments whose sound is produced by blowing air into a mouthpiece shaped like a cup or funnel. Tubas and trombones are brass instruments.

chamber music
Classical music written for a small group of musicians, so that it can be performed easily in a small room or private home.

choir
A group of people who sing together in a musical performance.

chord
A group of musical notes played together.

Latin American
From or relating to the countries of South America or Central America.

marching band
A group of musicians who incorporate some type of marching with their musical performance.

note
A single musical sound. A group of notes together make a chord.

orchestra
A large group of musicians who play many different instruments together. Members of an orchestra are led by a conductor.

pace
The speed at which something happens.

percussion
Musical instruments that are played by hitting them with your hand or an object such as a stick.

pitch
How high or low a musical note sounds.

samba
Music for dancing the samba, which is a type of Brazilian dance.

timbre
A quality of a sound that makes voices or musical instruments different from each other.

tuning peg
A short stick with a flat, rounded end that is turned to tighten or loosen the strings on an instrument.

vibration
A continuous quick, slight shaking movement.

vocal cords
A pair of folds near the top end of the throat whose edges move quickly backward and forward. They produce sounds when air from the lungs moves over them.

volume
How loud or soft music is.

woodwind
A group of pipe-shaped musical instruments that are played by blowing through a reed or a thin tube at one end or across a hole near one end. Flutes are woodwind instruments.

TOPIC WEB

Use this topic web to discover themes and ideas in subjects that are related to how musical instruments work.

Music
Listen to a piece of overtone singing. How does it sound different from the singing voices you know? Investigate how the voice box is used for this singing technique and draw a diagram to explain.

Science
Find out how our ears communicate vibrations from the air to the brain to make us hear music. Draw a labeled diagram to explain your findings.

Musical Instruments

English and Drama
Listen to two contrasting pieces of classical music. Think about how the use of different instruments makes you feel. How do the pitch, timbre, and volume affect the mood of each piece of music? Use one of the pieces as an inspiration to write your own poem.

History
In Tudor times, the lute was a popular musical instrument. Find out about the lute. What kind of instrument was it and how was it played? Compare the lute to the guitar.

INDEX AND FURTHER READING

Books

Digital Music: Computers That Make Music
by Ananda Mitra (Chelsea House Publications, 2010)

Is the Trumpet For You?
by Elaine Landau (Lerner Publications, 2010)

Master This: Guitar
by Seb Wesson (PowerKids Press, 2010)

The Science of a Rock Concert: Sound In Action
by Cathy Allen (Capstone Press, 2010)